The Well of Truth

What People Are Saying

"When reading, The Well of Truth, I found myself taking note of how attainable the author made having a better quality of life. This is not a Pollyannaish book of just being positive. The author clearly connects the dots of living purposefully and empowering people to grow in their lives. For me, this proactive approach to life is invaluable. It can, and most likely will be challenging to look inwards in such an honest manner, but the result will be worth it. My hope is that this is read with unconditional love towards oneself, and is understood to be a toolbox to live better lives."

- K. Jahanian, LMFT

"Here's a perfect gift for a friend or loved one who's troubled and struggling to find their pathway in the world. A lot of good advice is packed into this slim volume. Good thinking leads to good doing."

- J. Burke, Esq.

"I absolutely loved this book! It opened my eyes to how much negative thoughts effective my life daily, not only thoughts that arise from within, often times without even being consciously aware of them, but also external factors that create negative and unwholesome thoughts.

Since reading this great book, I wake up each morning with a positive affirmation, and a dedication to keep my awareness on my thoughts in the present moment. Already I have seen positive changes in my life by applying the principles laid out so clearly in this book. I highly recommend it!!"

- Johnny K.

"The Well of Truth is a book that everyone should read. It provides simple steps to think about what you let enter your mind. In particular, I enjoyed that it points out that each person is in charge of their own mental journey. Fate or circumstances do not dictate what you think, you do! Another aspect of the book that I enjoyed is the importance of Daily Affirmations. As the book points out, it seems so easy but is so difficult to do on a daily basis. I found the Well of Truth to be an inspiring book for so many parts of my life."

- Mike M.

"The complexity of the human mind is mysterious and staggering. This book does a phenomenal job of preparing us for the daily battle we all face. It provides great insight and wisdom to help all readers navigate through this complex and challenging journey! The author passionately articulates wonderful and positive insights of thinking that will yield purposeful and enlightened results. In my opinion, this is not a book you read just once!"

- Jered P.

"This book provides a direct, insightful and effective argument for the premise that one's emotions and consequent thoughts are the vehicle for one's actions. Those actions, beneficial or harmful, are then capable of being altered by the individual's own thought.

The author provides simple but ingenious techniques to mold thoughts into actions that reflect the positive. This book was immediately accessible at first read; leaving me to begin the process of employing this fascinating guide to self reflection and the fruits of the author's insights."

- Dr. G. MacWhorter

... see more at thewelloftruth.com.

The Well of Truth

the secret to living a better life

Mark Hastings

Contact us for bulk purchases, educational, business, or sales promotion use:

http://thewelloftruth.com

info@thewelloftruth.com

Published in the United States

by The Way Institute

ISBN-978-0-9985525-2-1

Version 1.1

For my love, I write this book to her first born,
Nathaniel

Table of Contents

Introduction

The truth of the universe is quite simple, really. You become what you think.

Every person has the power to create circumstances through the shaping of action brought forward by the person's own thoughts. Every single thought, whether good or bad, produces and shapes circumstances that produce either joy or displeasure. Every good, virtuous, noble, and pure thought will produce good action that in turn will create and reveal a good circumstance. Every bad, evil, sickly, selfish, weak, and sinful thought will, just as certainly, produce and reveal a bad circumstance.

Every thinking person is a living, ever-changing composite of good and bad thoughts. Every person's circumstances are also ever-changing, and the changes in circumstances are created through the application of, or the abuse of, good thoughts. Every grade of character is created through the accumulation of circumstances, and all lives are impacted by this truth. Those with predominantly bad thoughts live difficult lives of unwanted circumstances. Those with mostly good thoughts live pleasant lives blessed with joy.

Here's why this book is an excellent investment of your time: Understanding this truth will uncover a realization that every beautiful, desirable thing, whether spiritual or material, is attainable through the diligent use of pure, virtuous, righteous, and noble thought. Dreams, goals, aspirations, and wishes are all attainable when you become committed to a lifestyle of applying and practicing thought control.

If thoughts do not stem from love, truth, and compassion, or if thoughts are not noble, virtuous, and wholesome, they will fail to bring about desirable circumstances.

If you will honestly compare your thoughts to the highest, most noble and virtuous thoughts, and then if you will use self-control to re-shape your thoughts so that they become only wholesome, compassionate, loving, true, noble, and virtuous, you will certainly be astounded by how rapidly your circumstances will turn. Making this the daily pattern of your thought life will lead to consistently desirable results.

This strategy for life is nothing new. Many prophets, teachers, philosophers, and sages have taught these same laws for centuries. To the very few strong-minded people who bravely invest the challenging yet necessary hours to honest analysis and control of thought, dismissing all that is weak, selfish, impure, and base, they will be the blessed and fortunate ones who, by this great universal law, see shocking, immediate, and directly proportional effects on their circumstances.

This simple truth emerged after countless hours of concentrated thought, self-examination, meditation, and prayer. It has been proven both by analytical examination and through experience.

2

This is not intended to be one more book about "positive thinking."

The intent of this book is to demonstrate how correctly using conscious thought will develop a person's character and indirectly, but surely, shape and facilitate desirable circumstances in life.

By learning and using this information, you will gain insight into the elusive truth that allows for your complete mastery over destiny, creating what is desirable and dismissing all that is undesirable.

In this slim and straightforward volume, you will learn the true, undeviating law of the universe: All pure, good thought will produce good circumstances, and all bad thought will produce undesirable circumstances. Either way, your thoughts create all the circumstances you will ever face in life.

Success

Every person desires success. However, few people ever stop to define it. Many believe they understand success, but under close scrutiny, most people comprehend it to only a very limited and superficial extent.

Success is often equated with fortune or fame. This however, is not true success. Money, fame, prestige, and all material things cannot deliver true peace of mind. These fleeting, ephemeral things do not, in and of themselves, lead to self-awareness and spiritual harmony. It is a gross misunderstanding to think that fame, fortune, or any outside source could bring true happiness. Money cannot buy happiness, and large amounts of money, though it obviously relieves financial pressures, doesn't automatically bring happiness, relieve all suffering, or provide full contentment. It is superficial to imagine that making big money corrects undesirable circumstances.

Closely examined, suffering is always the result of persistent unwholesome thought, which produces unwanted circumstances that money cannot mitigate. Material wealth can only bring temporary pleasure, which by its very nature, always demands more. Since these pleasures can never bring true peace of mind, they fail to bring true success.

True success is only attained by the very few who understand that a virtuous life filled with love, truth, and compassion, and all that is pure, will reveal the desired circumstances of true success: joy, peace of mind, and serenity. True success shows up looking like this: there's a new sense of grace in your relationships, in your love, in your career, in your health, and in your purest, most desired aspirations.

Your purest aspirations – your highest, noblest unselfish dreams and goals – are eternal and spiritual. Contrary to the material possessions of life, these aspirations are items you can take with you. People everywhere understand that acquiring great wealth takes incredible amounts of focused thought, energy, and self-sacrifice. But what few people understand is that the pathway to true success is to apply these virtues to the spiritual world, not the material world. It is much more difficult to do, but the reward is a deeper, lasting, secure sense of success.

Pure, noble virtues will always deliver a wealth of joyful circumstances. This will lead to everlasting peace of mind, serenity, and grace. These are the true jewels of success. The one who understands this eternal truth will be able to look back over life with joy, understanding that correct efforts in thought are forever blessed.

No one can attain these beautiful spiritual qualities until understanding that thought forges all circumstances, and more importantly, all thought can and should be controlled. Understanding that thought can be controlled makes it possible to begin to control thought. Applying controlled thought to virtuous aspirations always produces favorable circumstances. Conversely, the abuse of thought consistently leads to unpleasant, undesirable circumstances.

You Are What You Think

You literally are what you think. You are always in the process of becoming what you're thinking about.

You are no more and no less than the sum of your thoughts. Many falsely believe their inner thoughts are secret, but every thought is clearly seen in the circumstance it produces. The supreme law of the universe is clear: no bad thought can produce a good outcome, and no pure and noble thought can produce a bad outcome. Although it seems simple to understand, reaping the value of this truth comes only to those who are willing to examine each and every thought, replacing bad for good. Successfully achieving this demands consistent effort and stark self-honesty. Each person is ultimately responsible for creating and shaping his or her life, circumstances, and destiny.

All thoughts emerge from emotions. Good emotions naturally spawn good thoughts. Bad emotions naturally spawn bad thoughts. Emotion spawns thoughts, and thoughts result in actions and habits that, either directly or indirectly, shape circumstances. Those circumstances become destiny.

This is the way of the universe. It works in no other way. Learning to apply good thoughts to any bad emotion using love, compassion, and truth comes only to those willing to dig deep in their souls, seeking the higher truth. It requires close scrutiny and extensive self-examination, but by applying noble, virtuous truth to every reactive emotion, one may overcome weak, selfish, petty, and negative thoughts. Only then is it possible to see every situation as a test – a test of grace. Grace is a supreme peace of mind that results from diligently-practiced thought control. Grace happens when reactionary emotion no longer controls thought. Grace happens when one is finally able to supplant anger with compassion, jealously with love, hate with understanding. Grace happens when one is able to use noble, virtuous reason instead of base and groveling thought. When you can control each and every thought, using pure, virtuous, compassionate, and loving reason, you will be astonished by the immediate transformation in your life. Now, the goals of attaining joy, peace of mind, serenity, and grace are well within reach. This is true success and the most reliable way to a spiritual heaven.

Many like to believe they suffer poor circumstances, or even a poor fate, because of other people. Though this appeals to our vanity, it is not true. No one can create a circumstance for anyone else. Each person is solely and directly responsible for the circumstances that person creates. If a circumstance is unpleasant, it is because the person creating it secretly harbors a deep-seated weak, selfish desire. People believe their secret, negative, groveling thoughts will not affect the material world of circumstance, but they are wrong. Every thought absolutely has its effect. If you suffer and wonder why, look for and examine the thoughts that created the suffering. If you honestly apply reflective reasoning as a way to understand unwanted circumstances, you will learn how to correct bad thoughts and by doing so, facilitate new, desirable circumstances.

Duplicity of Thought

Once you understand that thought is the direct shaper of all circumstance and that self-control coupled with careful watchfulness is the path to thought control, you can begin to practice self-awareness. There are many difficult challenges to overcome upon arriving at the threshold of practiced self-awareness and self-control. One of the biggest needing to be addressed is duplicity of thought.

Duplicity of thought arises from mixed emotions. Mixed emotions produce mixed thoughts. Purity of thought is only accomplished when there are no fractions of thought. Thought must be 100% pure to produce the delightful circumstances you seek. Those willing to exercise devout determination in honest self-analysis will soon discover duplicity of thought to be a great pitfall in the quest to align your thoughts with all that is right and good.

A thought that is impure will produce a circumstance that is impure. Cultivating all circumstances so that they bloom into a destiny of graceful opportunity requires your willingness to weed out any aspect of thought which secretly harbors intent other than what is right. Careless, irresponsible, unchallenged thought will fall prey to weak, emotional responses. Adrift, abandoned thought is quickly corrupted by the ever-present counterforces of evil, selfishness, groveling, and weakness that dwell within everyone. Only those who understand this will begin to possess the true strength necessary to elevate their thoughts to all that is wholesome, pure, and right at every opportunity. Once thought is purified and used wisely and correctly, all ensuing material circumstances will be delightful.

Justification

As you look deeper and deeper into yourself and as you begin to take the necessary time to analyze your thoughts, be acutely aware of that self-serving slayer of grace and peace of mind – justification. Justification is the mental process by which people give excuses and reasons through careless logic to explain and justify a wrong thought in any direction. Many people, claiming to understand the supreme law of purified thought, will fail to attain thought control as a consequence of justification. Good will not come from evil, no matter how we rationalize it, no matter how many excuses we think of, and no matter how many reasons we list. When that negative-resistance emotion pours out of you from a moment of testing – when during the moment of emotional reactivity negative thoughts come leaping forth and negative emotions surge – the supreme law reveals itself in unpleasant circumstances, and your constantly-changing life becomes shaped by suffering. Reactionary, emotional thinking that you falsely justify causes tremendous pain and distress. These tests can be a great teacher, though, because residing within this suffering is a divine opportunity to see and understand what thoughts have been secretly held inside our hearts.

As with animal instincts, all parts of ourselves that come from ego, vanity, and pride are forever straining to exalt their primal justification to be right. But what is right is right, and what is wrong is wrong. Justification of wrong for right, allowing a reactionary, unchecked, groveling thought to come forth, can never be right and can never be pure. We are fooling ourselves if we think a desirable circumstance is going to emerge from this kind of justification.

Prison of Thought

Wealth and status are poor indicators of true success. A person may rise to the pride and envy of an entire community. A person may have fortune and fame. A person may do many good and noble things. But that same person may suffer inside with depression and anxiety, and here's why: Since every thought produces its just reward in circumstance, even if a person has mostly good thoughts, that person's unwholesome thoughts will still bring unpleasantness and suffering.

Where do various kinds of thoughts lead you?

Thoughts of doubt lead to failure, disappointment, non-fulfillment, and destitution.

Thoughts of fear lead to anxiety, agitation, and failure.

Thought consumed by grievances leads to depression, loneliness, sorrow, and misery.

Judgmental thoughts lead to dramatic, explosive interactions with others, displeasure, and anger. Thoughts of greed lead to depression, corruption, crime, and anxiety.

Thoughts of anger lead to displeasure, violence, and crime.

Selfish thoughts lead to isolation, loneliness, and broken relationships.

Thoughts of pride lead to egotistical behavior, arrogance, and letdown.

Thoughts of envy lead to self-doubt, insecurity, anxiety, and disappointment.

Thoughts of self-entitlement lead to broken relationships, low self-esteem, and failure.

Thoughts of self-pity lead to selfishness, isolation, and loneliness.

Begrudging thoughts lead to depression, anxiety, and loneliness.

Each of these unwholesome trains of thought are signs of weakness, and each one leads to unhappiness, dejection, and misery – the opposite of blessedness. Wretchedness like this may be present in a person's life without obvious outward signs. Many people are wealthy and have material symbols of success yet have shattered personal lives of loneliness, grief, shame, and hopelessness. Others, though their lives may seem meager and frugal on the outside, are blessed with love, health, vitality, and joy.

Holding on to and cultivating good, healthy, virtuous thoughts is a sign of strength. These are the tools on which you can build a truly rich life of joy, with peace of mind and enduring relationships. Unwholesome thoughts are the instruments of both self-destruction and self-imprisonment, where the joy and peace of mind you seek is held captive. The few who work to build up more strength in self-control and purified thought will break free from this self-imprisonment. The more you examine your thought and work to replace unwholesome thought with good, virtuous thought, the more strength and peace of mind you will enjoy.

Some people find themselves unhappy with their station in life. They feel they are poorly compensated and under-appreciated. These people often sincerely believe they deserve more than what they are getting out of life, and they feel frustrated and unjustly victimized. The way out of this dilemma is to work in your own mind, patiently yet persistently focusing on love, compassion, virtue, and higher knowledge. You can escape the prison of your circumstances by freeing yourself from the prison of habitual bad thinking.

Soon, when you have reached a higher level of noble, virtuous, wholesome thought stemming from love, truth, and compassion, you can begin to look at every challenging circumstance as a learning opportunity – a chance to exercise your new skills of thinking correctly. Doing just that, and doing it consistently will free you from your unsatisfying station in life. You will find yourself so out of harmony with your poor circumstance, that it will be unable to hold you back any longer. What once seemed like a place of hopelessness will quickly blossom into rich opportunities for advancement, joy, and passion.

Another benefit of stepping out of the prison of poor thought is this: All people are attracted to beautiful, righteous thinking. Even people living completely out of harmony with themselves and others recognize virtuous thinking and respond favorably. When you right your thinking, you will become attractive and valuable to those around you, and this will create endless delightful opportunities for you.

You Are What You Eat

Your experiences – the things you do, the things you see, the things you hear – shape your thoughts. The human mind, some say, stores and remembers everything it sees and hears either consciously or unconsciously. The accumulation of all these stored images and sounds works to shape the inner personality of thoughts and emotions.

This idea goes on to suggest that the human mind is at the same time very delicate and quite resilient. Could you eliminate negative circumstances altogether by setting before your mind a diet of only beauty, for example, and avoiding everything base, violent, vulgar, or unwholesome? If your mind is shaped by what you see and hear and experience, wouldn't you be wise to exercise great caution in what you expose your mind to? Exposure to commercialism leaves you feeling inadequate, materialistic, envious, greedy, and insecure. Similarly, a diet of violence brings fear, anger, and resentment. Steadily consuming today's news media makes people fearful, skeptical, hopeless, despairing, and anxious.

Though you cannot control everything you see and hear, you can control the choices you make. Will you focus regularly on television, movies, the internet, and other media? It's your choice, but you would be wise to remember that media information and entertainment are always coupled with a secondary agenda to sell or persuade you. Television is an easy example, obviously a vehicle for commercials that sell self-esteem through affiliation with some product. Commercials tell you that you are inadequate without their product, but you will be happy and successful if you purchase and use their product. Though most of us understand this intuitively, we often fail to grasp the impact repeated exposure to commercials is having on our thoughts, emotions, and character. Just like television, magazines, newspapers, movie trailers, videos – every kind of media – have a secondary agenda like this, and the constant barrage of mind-dulling advertising has an extremely detrimental effect on thought. Even the content of movies and television shows leads to certain trains of thought. It's classic "garbage in, garbage out." What you expose your mind to greatly affects the way you think and the types of thoughts you have. You are what you think, and you will become what you continue to think about.

Your thoughts shape your reality and your circumstances. Be careful what you allow into your mind. Concentrate on things that are good, and the thoughts that come from what you see, hear, and read will be good thoughts that produce good, desirable circumstances.

Reality and Vision

Reality is what you think it is.

Each of us can recall a time when something bad happened, something that was very distressing at the time. Later, maybe after a lot of time passed, we came to understand that this was, in fact, a blessing. This is the very nature of "perception." Perception is how you interpret your reality in the present, not how it might have seemed in the past and not what you think it will be in the future. In fact, there is no past or future regarding your thoughts; there is only perception. Reality is the perception of what is occurring in the present. Perception changes as time goes on. Eventually, the unpleasant circumstances of today may be reinterpreted and remembered as tremendous opportunities for personal growth. So, the past is always changing, and the future is also always changing. Our thoughts create the future and become our reality.

If you stop and think about it, you will realize that right now – at the moment you are reading this – you are fine. The only challenge to you believing this truth is distress or anxiety you are remembering from some past, undesired circumstance or some distressing circumstance that you think will develop in the future.

The few who understand this and live in this reality experience serenity and peace of mind because they understand that, unless there is some direct, physical trauma displacing their sense of comfort, every person is absolutely fine at every moment of every day. How can you test this? Ask the simple question, "How am I right now?" The answer reveals that circumstance is nothing more than perception. Struggling against this truth is weak and immature. All undesirable circumstances, brought to life by impure, bad thoughts, are nothing more than a test. This test is this: Examining the suffering will reveal that it:

1. emerged from weak thinking
2. was self-inflicted
3. can be overcome by contrasting pure and good thought
4. will result in personal growth

The key to experiencing this growth is examining the cause and effect of thought. There is an eternal, divine creative force at work shaping your destiny as you continue to ascend to higher thinking using these tools.

Every circumstance starts as a vision, an imagining. Every great accomplishment starts with a well-crafted vision. If you want to achieve something great and lofty, or if you want your life circumstances to soar, you first need to understand the power of thought. Once you understand how directly linked your thoughts are to your goals, you can begin to create and exercise your vision. The more you intentionally use positive thoughts to create your specific, precise vision, the sooner that vision will become your present reality.

Every concentrated vision – either by choice and direct intent or by unattended, lazy, irresponsible thoughts –

will reveal itself to those who envision it. This is the true law of focused thought.

Finding yourself in very poor circumstances, then, is actually an arrival at your greatest hour of self-discovery. This abundant truth of focused thought will reveal itself. Once finished with vanity, pride, and ego, you can understand that your thoughts shape your destiny, and the poor state you were in directly resulted from your own mind. At last, having reached this crisis with this new understanding, you can come to realize that in your suffering was the elementary lesson for you of embracing right and eschewing wrong.

Your suffering, though self-inflicted, was there to teach you. Having learned how to think correctly, you can avoid future suffering. Recalling your suffering as a blessing can improve your current perception and lead you to a powerful vision for the future.

Discovering Self-Awareness

If you think about it, and if you are completely honest with yourself, you will realize that nothing happens as a result of fate and fate alone. It's easy to look around at other people and attribute their success to luck, fate, or good fortune. Though it may placate our egos, it is not true. Neither any great achievement nor any unfortunate setback happens as a direct result of fate. Instead, every achievement and every setback, no matter how big or how small, can be traced back to thought.

What happens to me is never the result of something you did, just as what happens to you is never the result of something I did. Blaming others is pointless because every circumstance we experience is the direct result of either consciously applied thought or unregulated, aimless thought.

Aimless thought is one of the great destroyers of serenity and peace of mind. To think aimlessly is to allow your animal instincts to control you. These thoughts are easy to recognize because they are full of selfishness: self-promotion, self-gratification, envy, greed, self-pity, fear and doubt. These thoughts, though you may not realize it, are capable of destroying any and all of your great desires and aspirations.

So, if the impact of fate is negligible, and if others are not controlling my destiny, and if my goals are being crushed by aimless thinking, what should I do?

Not everyone is ready yet to take the great steps of disciplined thought that lead to a destiny filled with purpose. For those who are just beginning to practice and learn the power of focused attention and thought but have yet to arrive at a developed vision for how to eliminate aimless thinking, the first thing to learn – the first great and important lesson – is self-awareness.

Self-awareness is the practice of doing every single thing with complete attention to the task at hand, no matter how insignificant the task may appear. Becoming present with every task, whether it's as simple as washing your hands or as complex as navigating group conflict, is greatly more empowering than aimless, mindless, thoughtless, perfunctory duties. Focusing your mind on each action forces you to stay in the present. It is here, in the present, that you can be aware of all your thoughts, banishing the weak, unwholesome thoughts and embracing the pure, good thoughts.

This unrelenting focus on the now spells the end of "mind-wandering." Though this may sound simple, it takes resolve, practice, and discipline. It is, however, the fundamental building block to gain the necessary tools that will bring about the great day when your dreams and goals – the ones you only recently thought were far out of reach – begin to become attainable. The beginning of controlling your thoughts is this practice of self-awareness. The good goals and high aspirations you have are certainly down this path because by controlling your thinking, you can create and shape your reality, your destiny.

This incredible power is well within your capabilities because you have the power to control what you think about. Accomplishments and achievements, whether of grand, global goals or personal, small dreams start with the practice of self-awareness.

The Great Jewel

Changing the way you think is going to take your constant effort, discipline, and practice, but it also comes with great rewards. Now that you are staying self-aware, firmly rooted in the present, and beginning to consciously recognize your thoughts, the next great step – and perhaps the most difficult step of all – is to begin to assign a value to every conscious thought. What is the root of each thought?

Is it rooted in virtue, compassion, love, truth, understanding? Is it noble? Or, is it rooted in envy, self-pity, greed, animal instinct, fear, doubt, or hate? Is it selfish and self-seeking?

Most people skip this and make no effort to apply a filter to their own thoughts. Assigning value to the source of your thoughts is one of the greatest steps you can take toward enlightened thinking. It's easy to be lazy and careless, letting your mind drift aimlessly, and it is tiring and difficult to force yourself to pay attention to every teeny-tiny thought. But the intense mental focus of linking the source of your thoughts to the cause and effect of your circumstances is like building a bridge to freedom. Yes, it takes dedication and focus, but when you are strong enough to do this, you will find yourself rightly conditioned – fully prepared – to create a great vision of success.

This great jewel of wisdom is right there for the taking, but it comes only to those who understand that in order to accomplish something life-changing, you have to be ready to struggle while you learn self-control and self-awareness, while you sacrifice taking the easy way in your thinking. Attaining greatness or simply achieving personal success requires that you put aside all lazy habits of aimless thought. No great accomplishment will come without being completely honest with yourself and holding yourself accountable to this new, high standard.

But here's the payoff. When you are able to honestly link every thought to its root emotion, you can begin to analyze every thought, and you will be astounded to find how easy it is to separate the right, good, noble thoughts from the base, selfish, poor thoughts. Now, at long last, you can harness the power of controlling your thoughts and shaping your circumstances. Now, you have no fear of personal responsibilities. In fact, you understand them better than ever. Like a jockey on a prize-winning thoroughbred, you are in control of your circumstances and responsibilities and can guide them wherever you wish. This is the great true law of purified right thought. It is the greatest power on earth, and you are now able to use it to take firm control of your destiny.

Reactive Thinking

Every day, no matter how much our own thinking is improving, we will hear others speak unfavorably and inappropriately. It is a considerable challenge, but one we must anticipate, to hold on to our own good, virtuous thoughts in the face of harsh, thoughtless remarks and actions of others. Having a workable strategy for this is important to think about ahead of time so that another person's raging torrent does not sweep you away. Remember, your thoughts are your thoughts. If bad thoughts originate with you or if they come to you as a reaction to someone else's words or actions, they are still bad thoughts.

We have already agreed that our thoughts, not fate, shape our circumstances and our destiny. We have accepted responsibility for our own future. We know that our thoughts have a cause-effect relationship on us and the achievement of our goals and dreams. That's why it's important to keep in mind that the reactive thoughts you allow in response to others will shape your circumstances just as certainly as the thoughts you allow in times of peace and quiet. Thoughts may come from appreciation of a beautiful vision, or they may come from a terse emotion brought on by the remarks or actions of another. Or, thoughts can come from aimless mental wandering. The great law of the universe does not play favorites. Each thought carries the power to shape circumstance and create change.

When others lash out with hatred, envy, greed, selfishness, harsh words, or other actions driven by their unguarded thinking, it is a reminder to us that their current and future undesirable circumstances have clearly come to them not through fate but as a result of a long line of poor thinking. Unknowingly, they have made their own bed, and now they must lie in it. To them, their thoughts and actions are completely justifiable and can be easily reasoned away or attributed to fate. In reality, though, it is their recklessness and their lack of self-control that have allowed their emotions to run rampant, resulting in thoughts and actions that are out of control.

Others act out because they suffer and because they have never understood that their unruliness stems from their own unwise choices. In these moments, you must exercise great self-control and strength of character to remain calm. You may have to consciously call to your mind that these people are encountering these situations as tests, that they are struggling but not understanding, and that they are either unaware or unconvinced that their own thoughts are to blame for their unfortunate circumstances.

The supreme purpose for adverse circumstances is to provide the necessary tests that allow people to grow and mature. For some, the tests will be easy. But for others, the tests will be difficult and frustrating. Your serenity and calmness in these situations will help you respond with compassion and sympathy, even if attacks or harsh words are directed at you.

Banishing weak, reactive thinking and taking the time to develop self-control are the foundations that will allow you to develop the ability to continually think higher, purer thoughts and dream great dreams. But developing pure, virtuous thought takes patience, practice, time, and great effort. Building the mind in strength and focus does not come by chance. Only by applying continual effort and by being very patient will you strengthen your mind until, at last, only beautiful and helpful thoughts remain.

Along the way as this effort progresses, even though you haven't mastered thought purification quite yet, it will be easy to start to see the link between cause (thoughts) and effect (circumstances), both in past and present experiences. The lightbulb of recognition is now burning brighter and brighter as the truth of thought purification becomes your reality.

As weakness gives way to strength, your circumstances will start to come into harmony with the purity of your thoughts and you will start to encounter delightful life opportunities. When you let go of your resistance, you will find other people starting to regard you with greater respect and acceptance. When you stop responding to other people's outbursts with negative thoughts and emotions and have replaced them with compassionate understanding, others will sense your internal strength and will desire it for themselves. You may even experience these people becoming softer and kinder and becoming interested in learning what you have learned.

Resistance and Acceptance

As we go together more deeply into our study of the enormous benefits of pure thinking, we arrive now at a lesson with tremendous power and usefulness. You've gained the important practice of self-awareness, and you have learned how to examine the root source of your emotions. But in your efforts to control your thoughts, you are discovering your own resistance, sometimes consciously and sometimes unconsciously.

Resistance comes from weakness in character, the mental and moral qualities that are distinctive to you. Loving, compassionate emotions and responses come from strength of character. No one is born with character; it's something you develop from the experiences of your life. It's something you build over time, often by working through difficult circumstances. As you concentrate your efforts on filtering out the demoralizing and useless thoughts, you will encounter your own resistance, and it will throw you right back into the test loop. But this isn't all bad.

Resistance is thought that is self-defeating, and resistance results in more unwanted tests. Though these tests are uncomfortable, they lead to helpful lessons that build positive character in you. So, resistance is really a test that leads to acceptance, and when you start to recognize this, you will have gained another step toward right thinking and lasting peace of mind. You have begun to accept what is.

Circumstances, you will begin to see, are neither bad nor good. No, they just are. Within every circumstance, whether desired or undesired, is an abundant opportunity for learning. If you find yourself resisting, take a step back and use your strength of character and your good, virtuous thinking to accept what is and look for the lesson masked in this resistance.

This is so powerful because, with this practice, you are identifying weaknesses within your character, examining them, and actually growing from them. Applying this practice is replacing weak character with new, pure, thought leading to strength of character. This will aid in the development of right thinking, and from this will come excellent opportunities.

Opportunity doesn't come by chance or by fate but from right thinking applied in a specific direction. Love and acceptance produce delightful circumstances. Resistance and weakness of thought produce displeasing circumstances, but their appearance tells us something within our character is missing and needs attention. Having discovered whatever was missing will lead to applying self-control in that area. Self-control, now applied to another area of your life, will bring with it the reliable fruit of pure thinking, serenity, and peace of mind.

Judging Others

In our quest to learn from our experiences, to remain self-aware, to identify the root source of our thoughts, and to sort through our own resistance, we will certainly come up against one of the biggest pitfalls in thinking – judgment of others. Judgmental thoughts of others are a trap we must avoid. More than that, we must work to do away with the habit of thinking this way.

Each of us, as we move around in our communities, are using our past experiences with people to form mental models of what we can expect from them. With someone new to us, our mental model often starts within seconds and is based almost completely on that person's outward appearance. It happens so quickly that it's like a reflex. Before you know it, you are judging this person in your mind.

Judgmental thinking is reactive, negative thinking deriving its source from our own aimless, unfocused thinking. Rendering judgment on someone without any basis in reality, without any interaction, without any real exchange of information, is a sign of a desensitized mind. This major pitfall in thinking is wrong and counterproductive. Judgmental thinking produces a reaction – an immediate, palpable tension – between us and the person we're judging. You may think your thoughts are secret, but the effect of your thoughts will not fail to produce circumstances, so in this way, your thoughts are not secret at all. Acceptance and judgment cannot coexist. Our struggle to gain purity of thought can have no greater proving ground than the battle between understanding with acceptance and the devastating error of judgmental thinking.

The greatest prophets and philosophers agree on this simple model behavior: "Do to others as you would have others do to you." Actions are always the product of thoughts. Your thoughts spur your actions, and your actions spur reactions from others. So, we can add an important prefix to this great model of behavior: "Think of others as you would have others think of you." This strategy elevates your thinking beyond the lazy, knee-jerk, judging-a-book-by-its-cover profiling of others into a place where you can begin to seek understanding and acceptance.

Judgmental thinking is a great destroyer of harmony and peace of mind, but when you have overcome your judgmental tendencies and begin to view others with understanding and acceptance, they will soften, and they will, in turn, become more accepting of you. This, now, is harmony. This is social interaction that brings peace.

It all starts with your mind. Your thoughts create your reality, and they run ahead of you, shaping the ever-developing circumstances of your life. If your thoughts are good – if you train yourself to think good, pure, virtuous, wholesome thoughts – they will build for you a life of delightful circumstances and opportunities. However, left aimless and unattended, you will lapse into the pitfall of judgmental thinking. If that way of thinking is allowed to continue, it will rush ahead of you to cancel your best opportunities and replace them with undesirable experiences and circumstances until through hardship you develop the character needed to avoid this pitfall.

Life is full of choices. A life of abundant opportunity and a delightful destiny awaits you if you will make the choice to pursue self-control by examining your thoughts and applied these concepts of right, pure thinking.

Self-Entitlement and Effect on Harmony

Another pothole to avoid on the road to enlightened thinking is self-entitlement, which is the erroneous belief that you are better or more important than someone else. This kind of thinking is a direct path to confrontation, anger, resentment, and injury. Nothing good comes from an attitude of self-entitlement. It destroys productive relationships and cancels all efforts toward success. Elevate yourself as someone superior by using some sort of justification or rationalization and it will rain friction, resistance, and frustration. When you look for harmony, you will only see an impenetrable barrier between yourself and right thinking.

Self-entitled thinking is actually a very reckless brand of ignorance born from pride, conceit, selfishness, and ego. By its very nature, self-entitled thinking cannot come from noble, wholesome, virtuous, loving, or compassionate thought. No success or desirable opportunity flows from it.

Instead, work in your thoughts to value others, because if you value other people, they will value you. All people deserve respect. To think great thoughts and achieve great success, you must understand that everyone is worthy of patience and respect. Everyone matters and every thought matters. Harmony with others born from good, pure thought is the supreme road to all that is desirable and worthy. When you work to be in harmony with others by demonstrating patience and compassionate understanding, you will find a new spirit of cooperation in them and your relationships will be infused with productivity.

Cooperation and harmony will take you to the fulfillment of your goals, dreams, and aspirations. Learning to recognize and identify your thoughts will help you root out self-entitled thinking.

The Most Powerful Force on Earth

Years ago, if someone had told me that I already possess the most powerful force on earth, I would have thought to myself, "Yeah, right!" I used to feel powerless to change the circumstances around me. I was convinced that my actions mattered little and my thoughts even less, since no one but me knew them. Perhaps this same sense of helplessness has taken root in your thinking. If it has, I want you to understand this one thing: YOU absolutely do already possess the most powerful force on earth, and it is your MIND.

Each human mind is – without a doubt – the most powerful force on earth for that person. Your mind has the power to create and destroy, the power for great good, and the power for terrible evil. Within your mind – within each human mind – lies the power to build up, to excel, to lead, to achieve, and to create. But also in every mind is the power to destroy, to hate, to murder, to avenge, and to self-destruct.

What difference does it make, you ask? You and your relationship with those closest to you shapes your family. Your family, in turn, shapes your community. Your community shapes your country, and your country shapes the ever-changing world. Each human mind, whether it is conscious of this or not, through either the concentrated effort to think positively and constructively or the willingness to allow mindlessness and negativity is changing the world we live in today.

You have rightly observed already that being successful at anything requires great concentration of thought. Academic success requires disciplined study. Success in business requires planning, trial and error, sacrifice, and all kinds of other focus. It's obvious that most people who accumulate great wealth have done it by great effort and sacrifice, so it should not surprise anyone that success in love, relationships, spiritual harmony, and knowledge is built the same way – through the concentrated devotion to using the most powerful force on earth – your mind.

Why would anyone be willing to make the necessary sacrifices to make money, but not for a romantic relationship, or a family relationship, or a spiritual aspiration, or even for good health? You don't have to accept failure in those areas.

The power of thought is the greatest power in the universe, and your mind is the most powerful force on earth. Using these two together is your express ticket to success. Do your life goals include a life of peace, a life with healthy loving relationships, a life of financial wealth, a life of good health? Those goals are achievable if you understand the power of your own mind and resolve to do the necessary work to control your thoughts and control your actions.

Now that you know this, you can do this. The more you work on it and learn about it, the better and stronger you will be able to do it. When you didn't know this, it seemed like there was no way you would ever be anywhere near achieving your goals, but now you can.

46

Right now – wherever you are as you read this – it's up to you to realize this: YOU CAN!

British philosopher James Allen once wrote, "Men are anxious to improve their circumstance yet unwilling to improve themselves." For you to have the life you want – a life you will look back on and smile about – you have to go after it. The power to change and to realize your goals and dreams and hopes is right before you. You can build for yourself the most beautiful life you can imagine because you have access to most powerful force on earth!

Before you is the door that's been closed and has been blocking you and keeping you from moving forward. It's swinging open for you right now. Walk through it, and see that on the other side, armed with the great law of the universe, you have the power to control your circumstances, to think beautiful, good, noble, virtuous thoughts, and to turn those thoughts into your reality, your future, your destiny.

It's the most important choice in life – to think with great noble purpose, or to let your thoughts drift carelessly and aimlessly wherever they would like. Think and dream a perfect life of peace and beauty, and it will be yours!

The Change

Making this change is not easy. It requires strength and courage because good and evil are going to collide in your mind. Every day. All the time. Good and evil flow from our thoughts, and they are strong forces that impact our own lives and the lives of others, but here is a comforting truth: the supreme law is always perfectly just, giving exactly (and only) what is earned by virtuous thought. Not so comforting is this corollary: the supreme law is also perfectly just regarding aimless or evil thought, bringing reality from those just as reliably as good circumstances come from good thought. The good news is that the effort to change will not go unrewarded. The bad news is that failure will also have its consequences.

Using the power of controlled pure thinking takes great patience and much practice. We will fail many times as we learn and re-learn the power of thought. Lowly, selfish, base, unwholesome thoughts will throw us back into unpleasant tests of grace, like we have discussed in previous sections. Good, pure, virtuous thoughts will create good circumstances for us.

How can you turn the tide and begin to experience more good, wholesome thoughts and outcomes and fewer failures and re-tests and unpleasant circumstances? The answer is to be honest with yourself and to own the results of your thoughts. Don't look to others as though they caused your suffering. Accept your circumstances and be honest with yourself that you – not anyone else –

created them and caused them. It has always been you, and it will always be you who creates your position in life.

But now, you have the power to change, and you have the knowledge to change. While it's true that a 1,000-mile journey starts with a single step, it's also still true that 1,000 miles is a long way. So remember, it's a marathon, not a sprint. It's a life habit, not a passing fad.

Changes will come every day, and every day you can practice and get better at purification of thought, becoming more and more aware of the thoughts you allow. Through success and through failure, you will see that you have the power to control and purify your thoughts, and that is the power to change your life. If you allow your mind to wander unattended, drifting aimlessly, the result will be undesirable. Aimless thoughts always fall below wholesome, noble, pure, good thoughts. If your life is a mixture of good and bad thoughts, your life's outcome will be a similar mix, and you can expect success in some areas and failure in others.

Life is always a choice. We all have the same ability to choose right thinking over lazy or evil thinking. Every time you choose right thinking, you are making a conscious effort to correctly shape your life. Good things happen to people who think good thoughts. It's that simple, and it's that challenging all at the same time.

How to Change

Knowing that electricity flows from power outlets does not make you an electrician. Similarly, understanding this universal truth does not, in itself, create change. Anyone can understand something, but having knowledge is not the same as using knowledge. People often read books and understand the concepts. They think that since they understand, the information will be magically or automatically applied to their lives. But most of the time, people file that knowledge away, even if they know it's good and helpful, and they keep living with what is familiar and routine.

Learning to use something new requires concentrated effort. Changing anything (but especially changing the way you think) requires a clear understanding that making this change is difficult.

Just a couple of basic things about the way our minds work may help us. For centuries, people have known about conscious thought and subconscious thought. Much of the brain is not utilized in conscious thought. The subconscious mind is always at work silently and beneath our own observation, crafting thought and shaping our conscious thought. The two are interdependent, always working together and influencing each other, but often without the other knowing about it. The subconscious mind affects the conscious mind's thoughts which, in turn, affect the words and actions that stem from thought.

Is it possible to learn to govern and direct our subconscious mind to aid in the objectives of our conscious mind? Could we create a cooperative union between the two of them?

Though very few have understood it and even fewer have actually used it, there is an age-old technique to use the vast, untapped power of the subconscious mind to facilitate the achievement of our goals. It is both powerful and miraculous, and incredibly, it's nothing new. What brings these two aspects of the mind into perfect harmony? Daily affirmations.

Daily affirmations have been used by the successful, the rich, and the famous for years and years. They have been used for noble purposes, and they have been used for immoral, unwholesome purposes. Either way, they work. Daily affirmations are specific goals that are written out and read out loud to yourself each and every day. They must be kept secret though; they cannot be shared with anyone else for any reason. If you share them, they lose their power to control your subconscious mind. Sharing them will also break the cooperative union between your conscious mind and your subconscious mind. It is fine to tell others you use the power of daily affirmations, but do not share the specific affirmations you are using.

Like any great thing worth pursuing, this is going to require great effort and personal responsibility. It may sound simple, but in fact, it will require advanced maturity and the resisting of our tendencies towards laziness. One of the keys to the success of daily affirmations is persistence. Think of daily affirmations as a daily patch repair for your brain. Daily affirmations correct the function of your brain, joining subconscious thought with conscious thought and unleashing the entire power of the human mind, the most powerful force on earth.

Written and recited daily affirmations are the very real facilitator of conscious visions. Having purified your thought and created a beautiful life vision, you can move toward this vision by writing down your specific goals. Affirmations must always be written as what is, not what is desired. A good example of a correctly-phrased daily affirmation is, "I speak only that which is true," not "I try to speak the truth."

When should you start using daily affirmations? You can start using them right away. You don't have to wait until your life vision is perfectly crafted. But you do need to make a commitment to yourself that once you start them, you will continue them every day, morning and evening, like clockwork. Please remember, daily affirmations are a daily prescription for your brain, and for them to work, they must be done daily.

The source for your first set of daily affirmations should come from you and your immediate goals. Here are just a few examples to help you begin thinking about how to write daily affirmations that will work for you.

Goal: *Improved peace of mind*

Sample Affirmation: I am so strong that nothing can disturb my peace of mind.

Goal: Moving on from the past

Sample Affirmation: I have forgotten the mistakes of the past and have pressed on to the greater achievements of the future.

Goal: *Being positive*

Sample Affirmation: I speak health, happiness, and prosperity to every person I meet.

Goal: *Stronger friendships*

Sample Affirmation: I make all my friends feel that there is something special in them.

Goal: *Being less critical*

Sample Affirmation: I give so much time to improving myself that I have no time to criticize others.

Goal: *Optimism*

Sample Affirmation: I look at the sunny side of everything and make all my optimism come true.

Another source of ideas for daily affirmations can be found by looking up *The Optimist's Creed.*

The number of daily affirmations you begin with should be manageable for you on a daily basis. Some people start with just a small handful, maybe three or four. As you begin to manage your thinking and become aware of your own areas of resistance, you will discover other areas where you need a daily statement to carry you forward in that area. So, the number of affirmations you recite each day is likely to grow as you go along. Seeing positive results often leads to some expansion, but be careful because it's so important that these are recited daily. If it becomes a long ordeal twice a day, people sometimes lose their commitment.

It is good to begin by reading and reciting your daily affirmations to yourself. Over time, you may wish to record them and play them back to yourself.

Once daily affirmations are created and used, always in secret, they direct the subconscious mind to begin working towards those ends. The subconscious never rests or sleeps but works continually, silently, in the background of the mind. You may be asleep, but this part of your mind never tires and never stops. It will work constantly until the object of its attention is attained.

The subconscious mind shapes thoughts and affects the words and actions coming from thoughts. Bad circumstances come from words and actions that originate with thoughts. Think of the problems we can avoid if we can avoid words that cause harm! When the subconscious is working with the conscious mind toward a goal, words will always come out more pleasantly, will be inoffensive, and will be received with pleasure. All this will happen automatically, outside of awareness, because the subconscious and the conscious mind are working together.

As it is with so many things, people want to change but are often unwilling to do the things necessary to change. Writing daily affirmations and diligently reading them aloud twice a day sounds easy, but very few will ever take on this exercise. It is so simple and so powerful, and though it requires maturity and persistence, it is not too difficult.

Controlling the subconscious and conscious mind is the very gateway to heaven on earth. Training yourself to take control and shape your circumstances and your destiny is no easy task, but it is possible through training, trial and error, and persistence. When you learn that this truth is the very real and exact way to accomplish your goals and have success in every aspect of your life, you will be happy to make these changes to your life.

Imagine having the body you desire, the love you desire, the career you desire. Imagine having joy and unwavering peace of mind. All these things are always available for those few who are willing to do the difficult task of learning and practicing thought control and self-control.

Peace of Mind

There can be no greater desire than peace of mind. Peace of mind comes from virtuous, noble, right thinking, and the correct pursuit of noble desires. It is the true indicator of real success. Most everyone chases after false success, on the constant trail of things other people admire. They are trying to satisfy their own vanity, and they are trying to look good to others. In the end, this trail arrives at a life of tragic circumstances, most often littered with broken relationships, sadness, corruption, disappointment, greed, and envy.

Peace of mind is the supreme state of mind that suffers no depression and no anxiety. It is the fine and perfect state that comes as a result of proactive, wholesome thought. The way to get there is to apply yourself to thinking good, noble thoughts that lead to desirable circumstances and success.

Peace of mind doesn't have a chance when humanity's raging passions struggle against unchecked emotions, leading to reckless reactions and circumstances that ruin lives. It's essential to look beyond mere pleasure seeking and materialism.

Peace of mind is another thing also – it's an indicator that you have reached self-awareness, where you choose your thoughts and choose your destiny. Self-awareness allows you to view each experience as a growth opportunity. When you start to look at life like this, you can see the good things everywhere you look. Now, your mind can relax and you can experience joy, living in the present completely aware and knowledgeable.

If self-control is not leading to the peace of mind you expect to find, if there's no serenity or calm despite your efforts at thought control, it's an indicator that something is wrong with your thinking. Take a closer look, make the needed corrections, and peace of mind will return to you.

Peace of mind is very attractive. All people follow and respect others possessing peace of mind. They may not even consciously understand what they're seeing, but people will instinctively desire to learn from someone who has this rare jewel of wisdom.

What's driving your ambitions and goals? Here's a challenge and an important requirement along the way to peace of mind: Honestly examine your motives. Look at your current desires and weigh them against the truth. Will attaining these goals provide you with joy and peace of mind? To think right is to be honest and to often ask yourself if your goals and dreams are born of wholesome, virtuous, noble thought. If they aren't, they will take you back through more tests of grace until your thinking has been purified.

Be well, use these words wisely; they are the very truth and the keys to all you could ever want.

"It is finished."

About the Author

Mark Hastings

This book has been a lifelong project for Mark. Growing up in a broken home, he discovered at an early age that his life was controlled by his thoughts. He figured out in his teens that changing his thoughts gave him the ability to change his life.

When he first put it into practice, he increased his sales 5-fold at his telemarketing job, claiming the top salesperson spot from that point on. In his early 20's, he used it to land a dream job in Hawaii diving and training dolphins, despite the fact he neither had a degree nor any diving experience.

Discovering a passion for helping people in his early 30's, he used it to graduate among the top of his class as a doctor - even though school was always a challenge before that. And he's parlayed that into the life of his dreams. He works just 16 hours a week, owns a beautiful house on 10 acres in the mountains with his wife, has a vacation home in Fiji, earned his commercial pilot's license, is an ordained minister, and actively gives back to his community.

Conducting more than 50,000 patient interviews over the last 20 plus years, he met people of all ages and from all walks of life. Most confided with him, not just about their physical ailments, but about the most personal aspects of their life.

He found that most people fell into one of two groups: those who were satisfied with their life and those who were unhappy with it. He wondered if a person who was unhappy with their life could change it - and what was necessary for everyone to succeed and be happy with their life. He recalled his personal journey. He read numerous books. He distilled it all into a simple set of steps that will work for anyone. He then wrote the Well of Truth to share this secret. He's confident it'll help you live a better life.

Learn more about Mark at thewelloftruth.com

One Last Thing

If you enjoyed this book or found it useful - please post a short review on Amazon. Your support and reviews make a huge difference making this and future books better.

Thank you!

Made in the USA
Las Vegas, NV
26 October 2022

58168967R00046